MY BODY Inside and Out!

What Happens When I Eat?

by Ruth Owen

Consultant:

Suzy Gazlay, MA
Recipient, Presidential Award for Excellence in Science Teaching

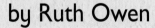

Ruby Tuesday Books

Published in 2014 by Ruby Tuesday Books Ltd.

Editor: Mark J. Sachner
Designer: Emma Randall

Photo credits:
Science Photo Library: 9 (top left), 14. Shutterstock: 1, 4–5,
6, 8–9 (bottom), 10–11, 12–13, 15, 16–17, 18–19, 20–21, 23.
Superstock: Cover, 7, 9 (top right), 17.

Library of Congress Control Number: 2013908616

ISBN 978-1-909673-26-7

Printed and published in the United States of America

For further information including rights and permissions
requests, please contact our Customer Service Department
at 877-337-8577.

Contents

Words shown in **bold** in the text are
explained in the glossary.

My Food's Incredible Journey

Every year, you probably munch through hundreds of sandwiches, bowls of cereal, and pieces of fruit.

It's hard to imagine, but every bite of food you eat goes on an incredible journey.

Inside your body, that food becomes **fuel** to keep you thinking, talking, moving, and playing.

What actually happens to food, though, once it's inside you? Let's check it out.

What happens when I eat?

The Journey Begins

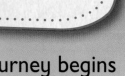

Did you know your food's journey begins when you see, smell, or think about food?

Before you even take a bite, your brain tells your mouth and **stomach** to get ready.

Your mouth starts producing a slimy liquid called **saliva**, or spit.

Once the food is in your mouth, your teeth cut and chew it into small pieces.

Your teeth and tongue work together to mix the chewed-up food with saliva.

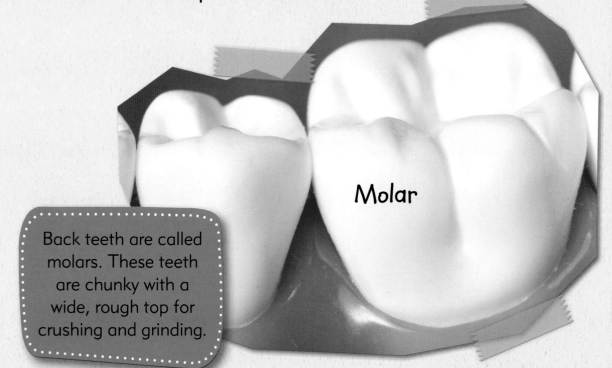

Molar

Back teeth are called molars. These teeth are chunky with a wide, rough top for crushing and grinding.

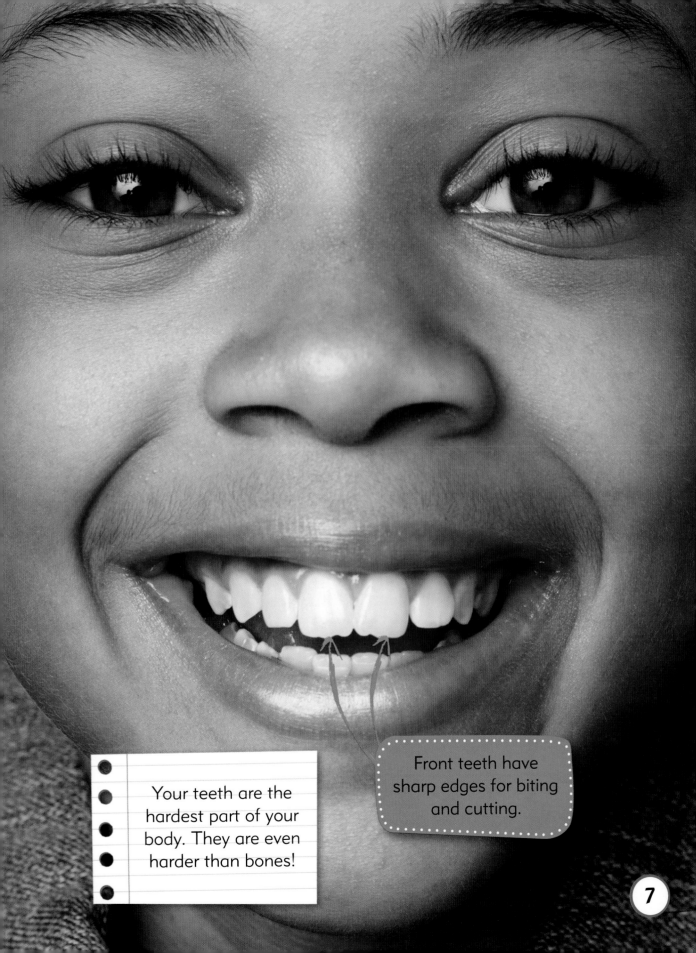

Your teeth are the hardest part of your body. They are even harder than bones!

Front teeth have sharp edges for biting and cutting.

Tongues and Taste Buds

As you chew your food, tiny **taste buds** on your tongue **detect** different flavors.

At the same time, your nose is smelling your food.

Your tongue and nose work as partners to help you taste your food.

That's why you sometimes can't taste your food when you have a cold.

Your taste buds are working, but your blocked nose can't smell, and can't do its job.

There are five types of flavors, sweet, salty, sour, bitter, and umami.

Different parts of your tongue detect different flavors.

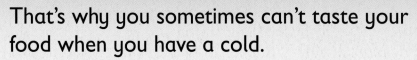

Tongue

Bitter

Sour

Sour

Umami

Salty

Salty

Sweet

Sweet

Ice cream

Chocolate

If you looked at your tongue under a microscope, this is what you would see. There are about 10,000 taste buds on your tongue.

Taste buds

Salty

Potato chips

Popcorn

Sour

Lemons

Grapes

Bitter

Coffee

Unsweetened cocoa

Umami

Meat

Mushrooms

Your Food Is On Its Way

Inside your mouth, your teeth and tongue turn a mouthful of food into a mushy ball.

Then you swallow the ball of food.

The **muscles** in your throat push the food into a long tube called the **esophagus**.

Inside your esophagus, there are more muscles.

These muscles push the food down the tube toward your stomach.

The ball of chewed-up food and saliva is called a bolus (BOH-luhss).

Bolus

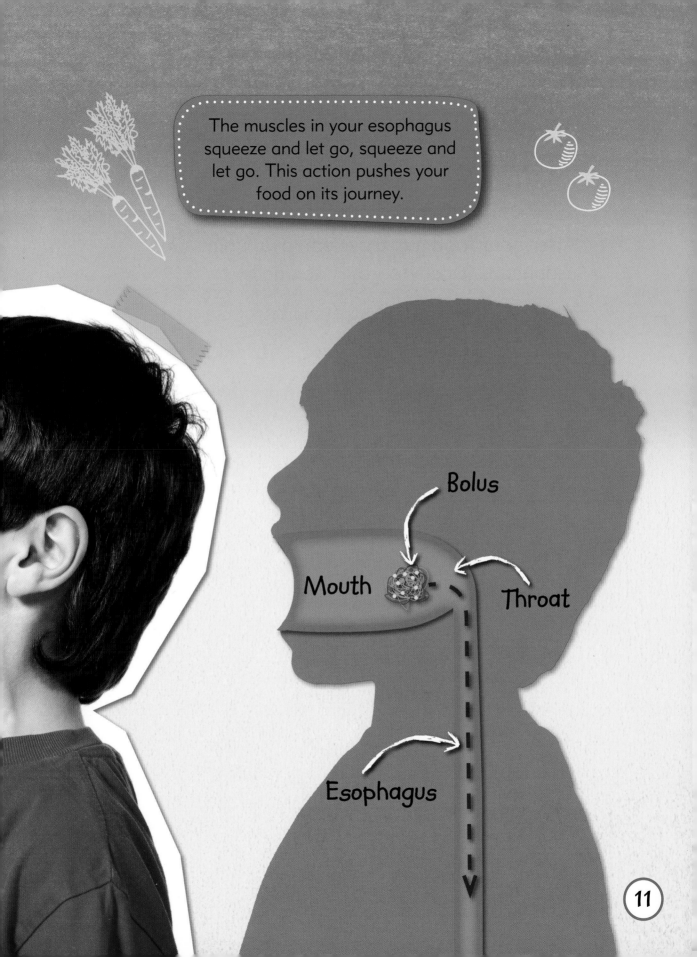

The muscles in your esophagus squeeze and let go, squeeze and let go. This action pushes your food on its journey.

Bolus

Mouth

Throat

Esophagus

Inside Your Stomach

After your food has traveled down your esophagus, it gets to your stomach.

Your stomach is like a stretchy bag.

It produces juices that **digest**, or break down, food.

Muscles in your stomach churn and mix your food with these juices.

After about three hours in your stomach, your food looks like a thick milkshake.

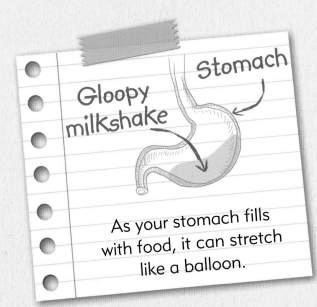

Gloopy milkshake

Stomach

As your stomach fills with food, it can stretch like a balloon.

Your stomach's large neighbor is the **liver**. This body part does hundreds of different jobs. For example, it keeps your blood healthy, and it stores some of the fuel that your body makes.

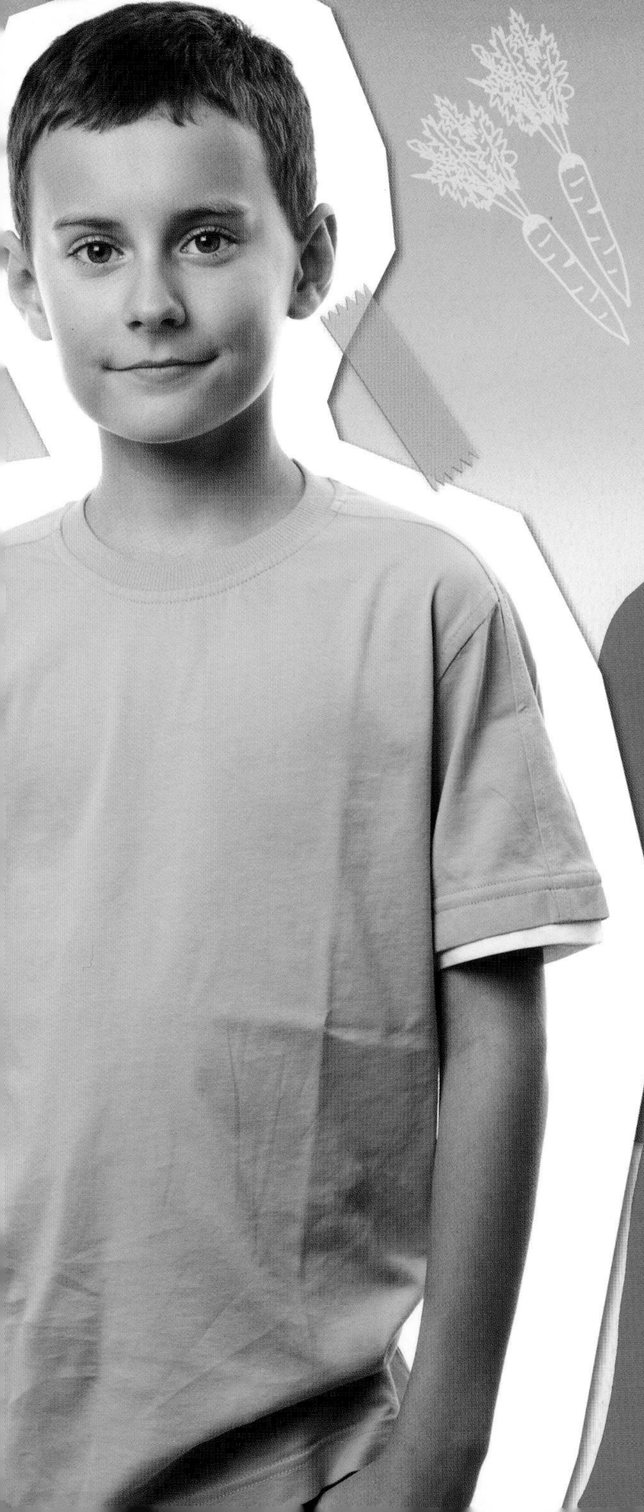

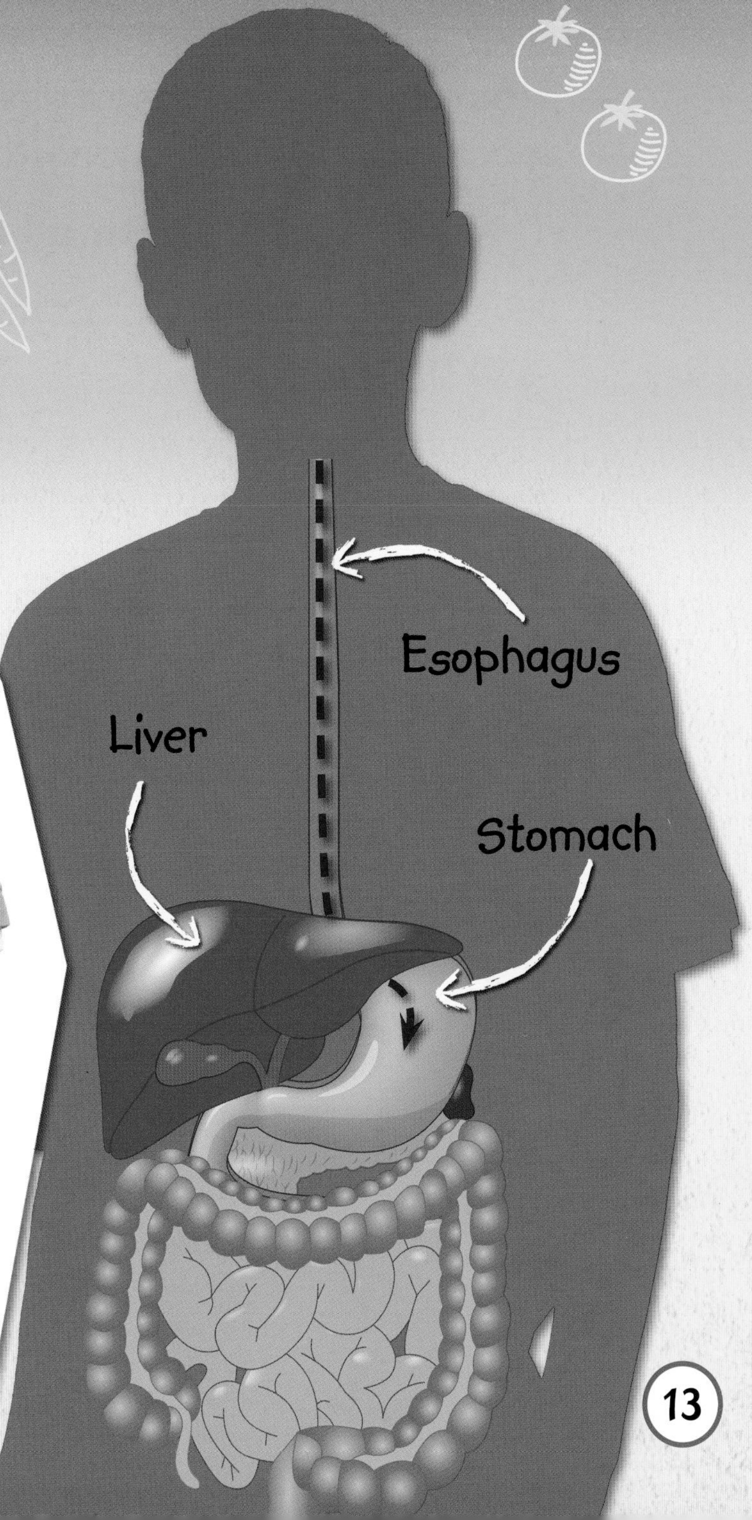

Esophagus

Liver

Stomach

Gathering the Goodness

From your stomach, the milkshake-like food mix moves into a long, thin tube.

This tube is called the **small intestine**.

Juices from the small intestine are squirted onto the food.

The juices break down the food so that the **nutrients** in the food are released.

The inside of the small intestine is covered with millions of tiny parts called **villi**.

The villi soak up the nutrients and then release them into your blood.

This is a close-up photo of villi from inside a person's small intestine. A microscope was used to zoom in on the villi.

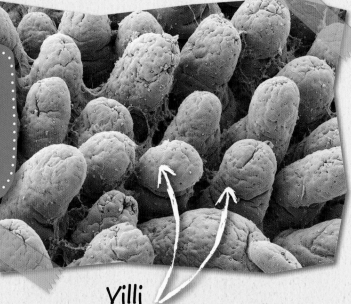

Villi

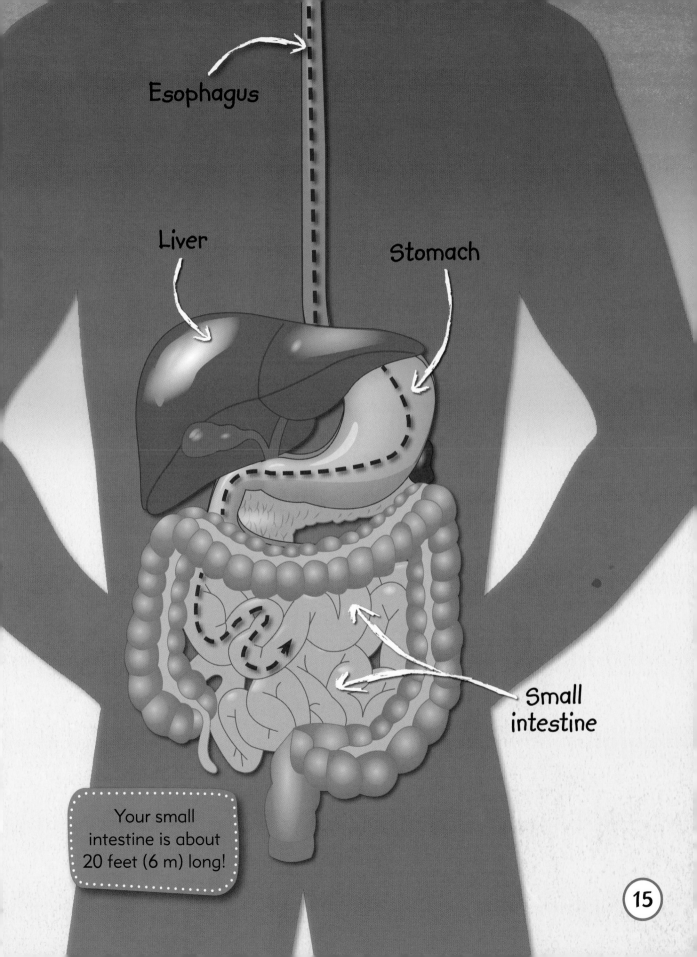

Esophagus

Liver

Stomach

Small
intestine

Your small
intestine is about
20 feet (6 m) long!

15

Your Food and You

The nutrients from your food are carried around your body in your blood.

Your blood takes the nutrients to where they are needed.

Some nutrients give you energy to move around, play sports, and do schoolwork.

Others help your bones, muscles, teeth, and hair grow.

Vitamins are nutrients that help your body fight off colds and other illnesses.

Your body needs water to be healthy. Along with nutrients, your small intestine soaks up the water you drink and water from your food. Then your blood carries the water around your body.

The End of the Journey

After the nutrients have moved from your small intestine into your blood, there is hardly any food left.

All that remains of your food are solid leftovers that your body doesn't need.

Muscles in the small intestine push these leftovers into a wider tube called the **large intestine**.

This tube soaks up any water still in the leftovers and releases it into your body.

The leftovers leave your body as poop when you go to the bathroom.

Every day, your body uses water from the things you eat and drink. When it has used what it needs, leftover liquids leave your body when you pee.

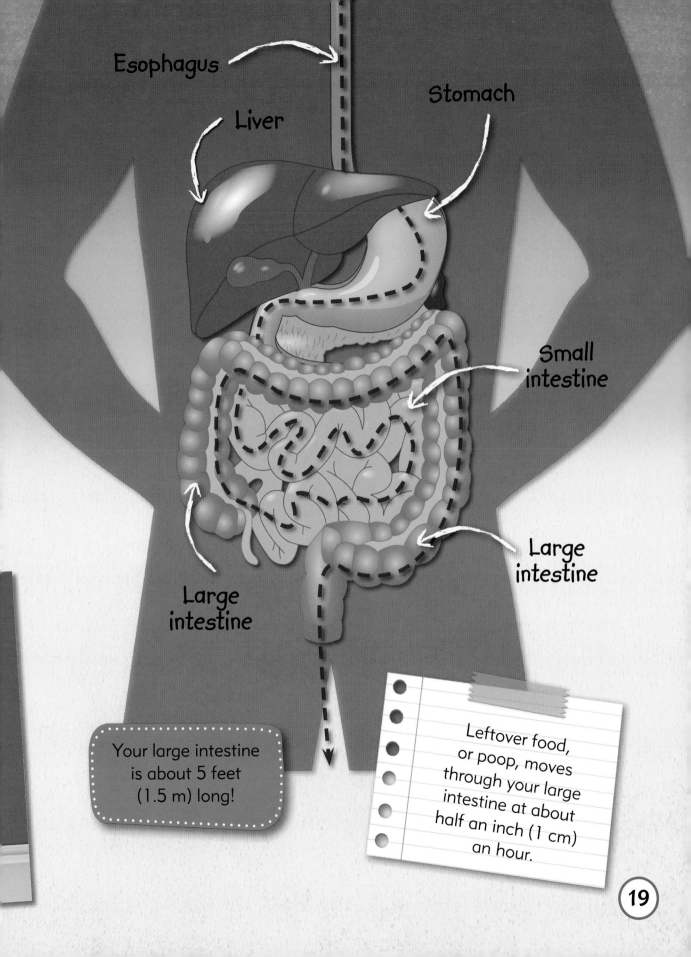

Esophagus

Liver

Stomach

Small intestine

Large intestine

Large intestine

Your large intestine is about 5 feet (1.5 m) long!

Leftover food, or poop, moves through your large intestine at about half an inch (1 cm) an hour.

19

Eating and Your Brain

Inside your body, your **digestive system** turns food into fuel.

There's one important body part that makes this possible, and that's your brain.

Your brain sends instructions to different parts of your body along pathways called **nerves**.

Body parts then send messages back to the brain.

From chewing to pooping, your brain controls everything that happens in your body!

It can take up to 30 hours for food to travel through your digestive system.

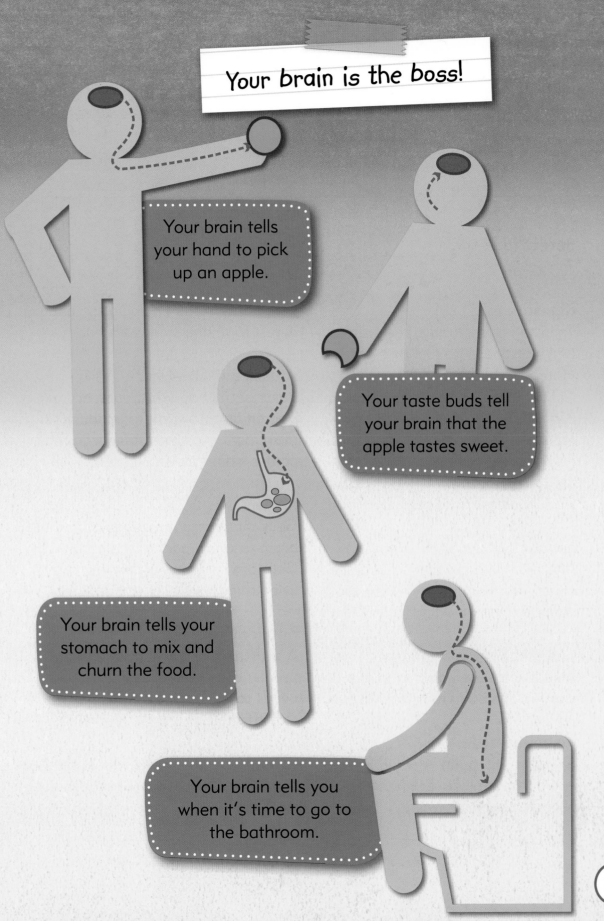

Glossary

detect (dee-TECT)
To recognize or identify something.

digest (dy-JEST)
To break down food in the stomach and intestines into fuel that can be used by the body.

digestive system
(dy-JES-tiv SIS-tem)
All the body parts, such as your mouth, stomach, and intestines, that work together to digest your food.

esophagus (ee-SAH-fuh-guhss)
A tube through which food passes on its way from the throat to the stomach.

fuel (FYOOL)
A substance used as a source of energy. The body uses food as fuel.

large intestine
(LARJ in-TES-tuhn)
A tube where leftover food becomes poop, or waste.

liver (LIH-vuhr)
A body part that does many important jobs, such as keeping the blood healthy and helping the body digest food and store nutrients.

muscles (MUH-suhlz)
Parts of the body that contract, or tighten up, and relax to produce movement. Muscles use energy that comes from food.

nerves (NURVZ)
Cells that carry messages from the brain to every part of the body. Cells are very tiny parts of a living thing.

nutrient (NOO-tree-uhnt)
A substance taken in by the body, usually through food, that the body needs to grow, get energy, and stay healthy.

saliva (suh-LY-vuh) A liquid in the mouth that helps us chew and swallow.

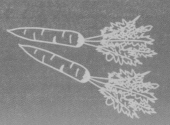

small intestine
(SMAWL in-TES-tuhn)
A long tube where digestion takes place after food leaves the stomach.

stomach (STUH-muhk)
A stretchy body part where chewed food is broken down by juices and then moved on to the small intestine.

taste buds (TAYST BUHDZ)
Tiny bumps on the tongue and elsewhere in the mouth that allow us to taste the flavor of food.

villi (VIHL-eye)
Small, fingerlike folds in the wall of the small intestine that soak up nutrients and release them into the blood.

vitamins (VY-tuh-minz)
Nutrients provided by food that are important to the body's health and growth.

Index

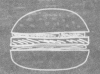

Read More

Prior, Jennifer.
The Digestive System (TIME For Kids Readers). Huntington Beach, CA: Teacher Created Materials (2012).

Showers, Paul.
What Happens to a Hamburger? (Let's-Read-and-Find-Out Science). New York: HarperCollins (2001).

Learn More Online

To learn more about what happens when you eat, go to
www.rubytuesdaybooks.com/mybodyeat